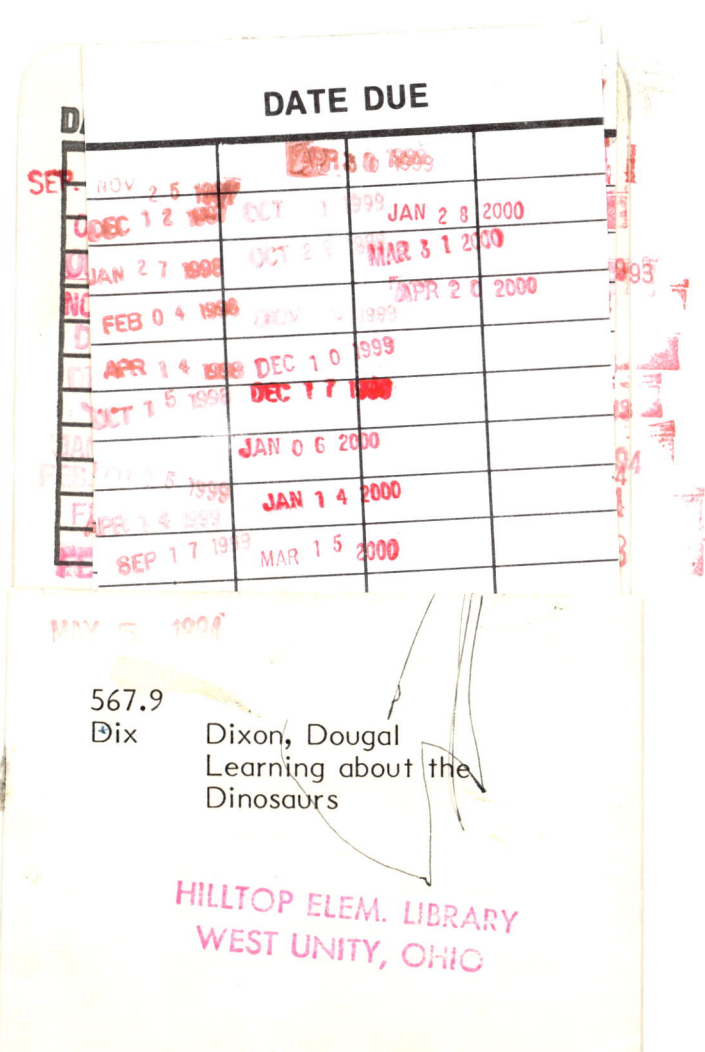

Learning about the
DINOSAURS

For a free color catalog describing Gareth Stevens' list
of high-quality children's books call 1-800-341-3569

Library of Congress Cataloging-in-Publication Data

Dixon, Dougal.
   Learning about the dinosaurs / photography by Jane Burton; text by Dougal Dixon;
artwork by Alan Male & Steve Kirk.
      p. cm. -- (My first dinosaur library)
   Bibliography: p.
   Includes index.
   Summary: Examines how paleontologists discover, study, classify, reconstruct,
and restore the fossil remains of many kinds of dinosaurs.
   ISBN 0-8368-0150-4
   1. Dinosaurs--Juvenile literature. 2. Paleontology--Juvenile literature.
[1. Dinosaurs. 2. Paleontology. 3. Fossils.]   I. Burton, Jane, ill. II. Male, Alan, ill.
III. Kirk, Steve, ill. IV. Title. V. Series.
QE862.D5D546   1989   567.9'1--dc20   89-4544

This North American edition first published in 1989 by
Gareth Stevens Children's Books
RiverCenter Building, Suite 201
1555 North RiverCenter Drive
Milwaukee, Wisconsin 53212, USA

This US edition copyright © 1989. Adapted from *Hunting the Dinosaurs*, which was based
on *The Age of Dinosaurs*, by Jane Burton and Dougal Dixon. Conceived and produced by
Eddison/Sadd Editions, London. First published in the United Kingdom and Australia by
Sphere Books, London, 1984, and in the United States under the title *Time Exposure*, by
Beaufort Books, New York, 1984.

Copyright © 1989 this format by Gareth Stevens, Inc. Artwork illustrations copyright
© 1984 by Eddison/Sadd Editions. Photographs copyright © 1984 by Jane Burton/Bruce
Coleman. Additional material and illustrations copyright © 1987 by Gareth Stevens, Inc.

All rights reserved. No part of this book may be reproduced in any form or by any means
without permission in writing from Gareth Stevens, Inc.

Series Editor: Valerie Weber
Editor: Julie Brown

Printed in the United States of America

1 2 3 4 5 6 7 8 9 96 95 94 93 92 91 90 89

Learning about the
DINOSAURS

Photography by
Jane Burton

Text by
Dougal Dixon

Artwork by
Alan Male & Steve Kirk

Gareth Stevens Children's Books
MILWAUKEE

Learning about the
DINOSAURS

The Very First
DINOSAURS

When
DINOSAURS
Ruled the Earth

The Last of the
DINOSAURS

Learning about the Dinosaurs

Looking at the skeleton of a prehistoric animal makes us wonder about many things. What did the Earth look like when the dinosaurs were alive? What did the dinosaurs look like? Why did they die out?

This book is about these and other questions. It is also about how scientists discover and put together the remains of thousands of extinct animals.

CONTENTS

Introduction 6
The Changing Earth 7
Plant Life on the Earth 8
Animal Life on the Earth 10
What Is a Reptile? 12
Running and Flying 14
Swimming and Burrowing 16
Scientists Study the Dinosaurs 18
Reconstructions and Restorations 20
A Museum Restoration 22
A Photographic Restoration 23
The Discoveries 24

Fun Facts about Dinosaur and Animal Life 28
More Books about Dinosaurs 29
Where to See the Dinosaurs 29
New Words 30
Index and Pronunciation Guide 32

Note to the reader: When you read this book, you will find certain words appearing in **bold type**. This means the word is listed in the "New Words" section on pages 30 and 31.

INTRODUCTION

Have you ever seen the skeleton of a dinosaur? Did you wonder what the dinosaur looked like when it was alive?

Dinosaurs first appeared on Earth 225 million years ago. They became **extinct** 65 million years ago.

The remains of these extinct animals are called **fossils**. Scientists who study these remains are called **paleontologists**.

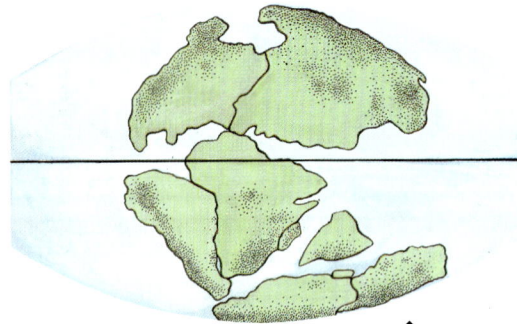 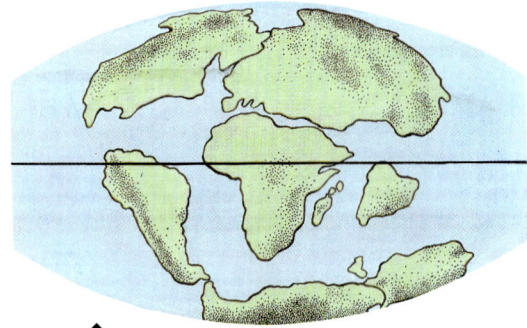

(1) Long ago, the continents were joined together like a puzzle.

(2) Later, they drifted apart.

THE CHANGING EARTH

Our planet is 4.6 billion years old. It has changed in many ways.

Continents are huge rafts of rock that float over the surface of the Earth. They are still moving. The deserts, rivers, lakes, and forests that we see today were also different when dinosaurs **roamed** the planet.

The blue on this map shows the areas of North America that were once under water. ▶

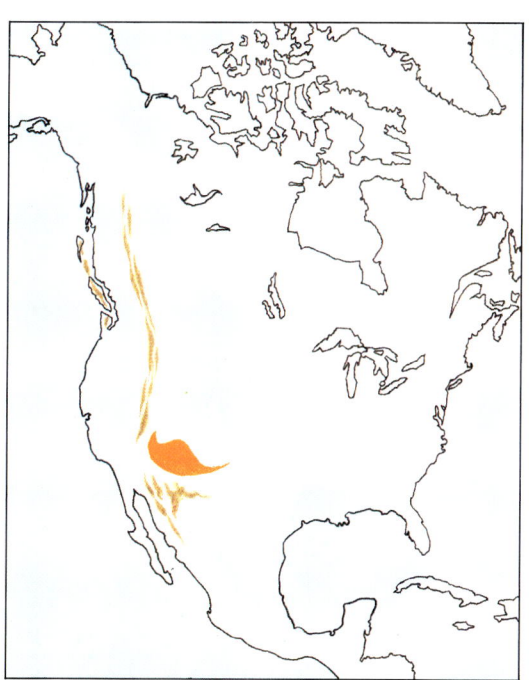

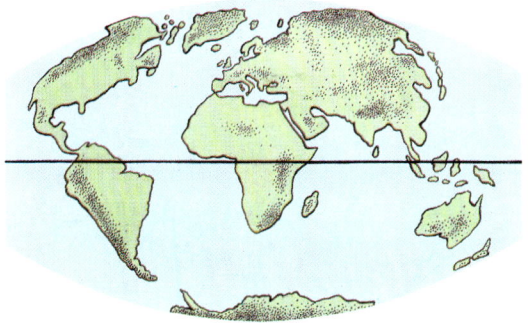

(3) They are still slowly drifting today.

7

PLANT LIFE ON THE EARTH

Plant fossils can tell us what plants looked like millions of years ago.

During the Age of Dinosaurs, plants were different than they are today. But like today's plants, they also needed soil, light, and water to grow.

These psilophytes are an early group of plants. They grew near rivers.

The first forests consisted of ferns and horsetails. Some of these plants grew almost as tall as a nine-story building. Later, flowering plants grew. Last of all came grasses. Many plants are now extinct, just like the dinosaurs.

Here are several ancient plants:
(1) fern, (2) grass,
(3) cooksonia, (4) horsetail.

ANIMAL LIFE ON THE EARTH

Over millions of years, animals have changed in many ways. The first animals were single cells, too small for us to see. They lived in the ocean. These single-celled animals slowly **evolved** into fish. As the lakes dried up, fish evolved into animals with lungs and legs to crawl on the land.

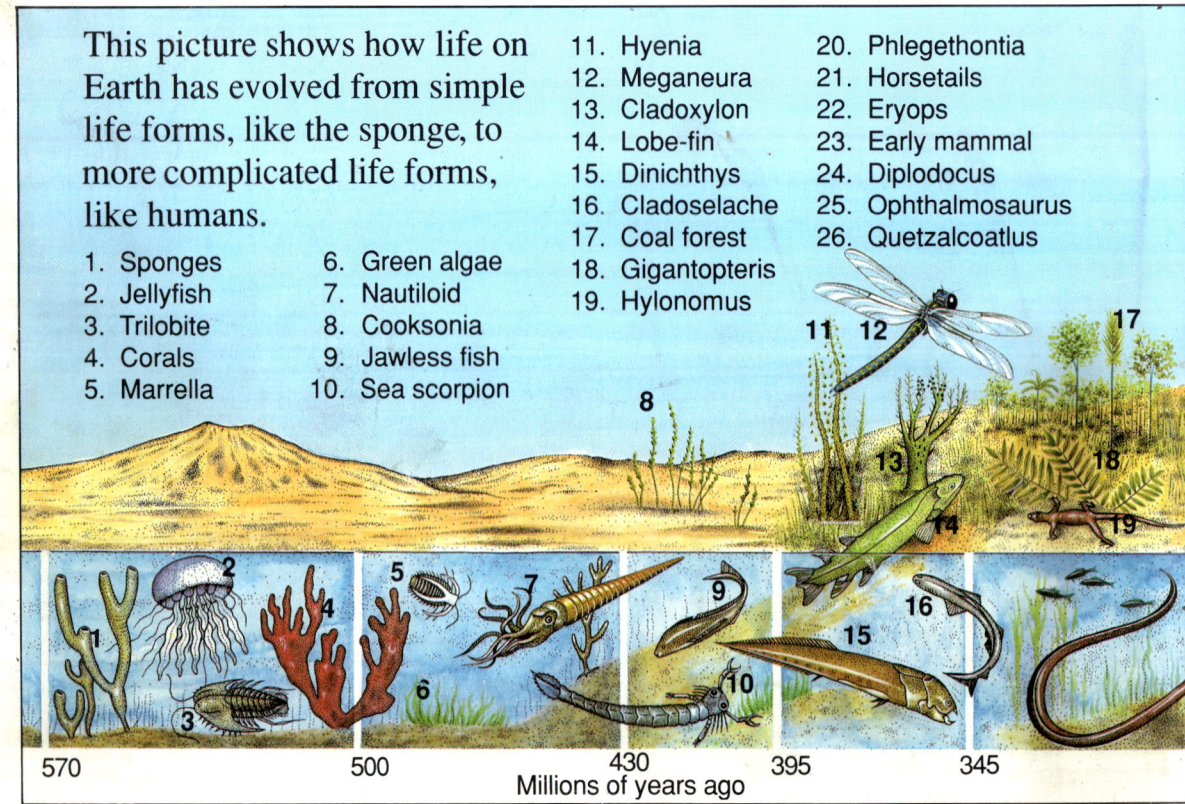

This picture shows how life on Earth has evolved from simple life forms, like the sponge, to more complicated life forms, like humans.

1. Sponges
2. Jellyfish
3. Trilobite
4. Corals
5. Marrella
6. Green algae
7. Nautiloid
8. Cooksonia
9. Jawless fish
10. Sea scorpion
11. Hyenia
12. Meganeura
13. Cladoxylon
14. Lobe-fin
15. Dinichthys
16. Cladoselache
17. Coal forest
18. Gigantopteris
19. Hylonomus
20. Phlegethontia
21. Horsetails
22. Eryops
23. Early mammal
24. Diplodocus
25. Ophthalmosaurus
26. Quetzalcoatlus

Reptiles also evolved on land. They could breathe air and walk. They laid their eggs on dry land. One group of reptiles became **mammal**-like animals. Before dying out, they gave rise to the mammals.

The first mammals were small. After the dinosaurs died, larger mammals, including humans, evolved.

27. Tyrannosaurus
28. Hesperornis
29. Toxodon
30. Desmostylus
31. Human

The Age of Dinosaurs

11

WHAT IS A REPTILE?

A reptile is an animal that lays its eggs on land. It cannot control its body temperature, so we call it "**cold-blooded**." It has scaly or horny skin.

Today's reptiles include crocodiles, snakes, lizards, and turtles. Millions of years ago, reptiles ruled the Earth. But they don't anymore.

Some people think all early reptiles were dinosaurs, but dinosaurs were only one group of reptiles.

The chart on the next page shows how certain animals of today evolved. For example, crocodiles and birds of today evolved from an earlier group of animals called thecodonts.

Euparkeria was one kind of thecodont that evolved into the dinosaurs. ▶

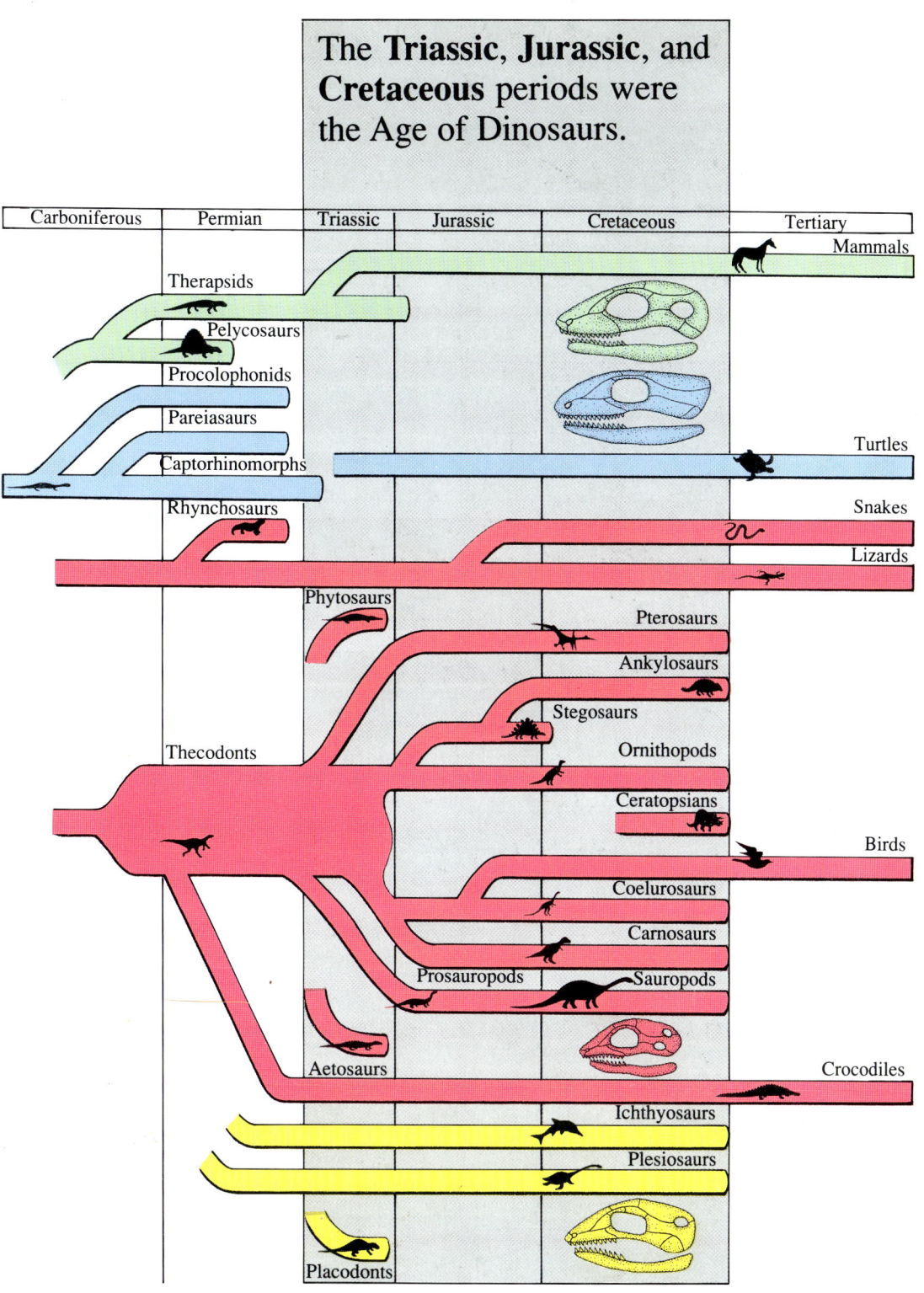

RUNNING AND FLYING

Animals that live in open spaces have few places to hide. That is why they must be able to move quickly. Long legs and a light body help an animal run fast.

Today's ostrich (left) and Struthiomimus (right) both lived in open spaces. See how alike their bodies are.

Flying animals need wings and a very light body. Flying uses a lot of energy, so they also need a way to control their body temperature. Feathers help with this.

What works for today's animals worked in the past, too. Scientists can tell what an ancient animal could do by looking at its skeleton.

Here are the skeletons of a pigeon (left) and a Pterodactylus (right). Both have wings and very light bones.

The dolphin (1), shark (2), and ichthyosaur (3) all had **streamlined** bodies and a fin at the tail.

SWIMMING AND BURROWING

An animal that lives in the water or in the soil must also **adapt** to where it lives.

Like certain animals of today, ancient animals that lived in the water had fins. They helped the animals steer. These animals also had pointed teeth for catching other sea animals.

Ancient burrowing animals needed sturdy bodies for tunneling through soil or sand. They had legs they could wiggle like paddles.

Moles (left) and skinks (right) are burrowing animals of today.

17

SCIENTISTS STUDY THE DINOSAURS

Iguanodon was one of the earliest dinosaurs to be discovered. In the 1820s, Gideon and Mary Mantell found the teeth and bones of an Iguanodon. They thought the animal would look like an enormous lizard.

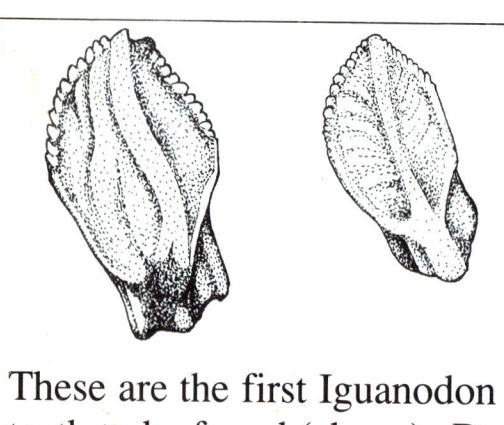

These are the first Iguanodon teeth to be found (above). Dr. Mantell thought Iguanodon walked on all fours (below).

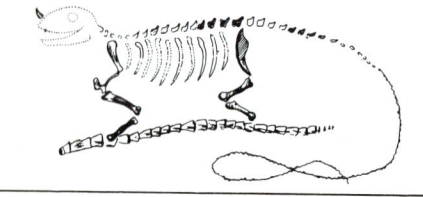

Later scientists thought Iguanodon was **warm-blooded** and ran swiftly.

In 1878, people found Iguanodon skeletons in a coal mine. Scientists learned from these that Iguanodon walked on its hind legs. Scientists continue to learn more about this mysterious animal.

Most models today show that Iguanodon stood on two legs.

RECONSTRUCTIONS AND RESTORATIONS

When a skeleton is pieced together, we call it a **reconstruction**. Old bones are very fragile and must be handled gently.

A **restoration** shows what the whole animal may have looked like, complete with skin and bones.

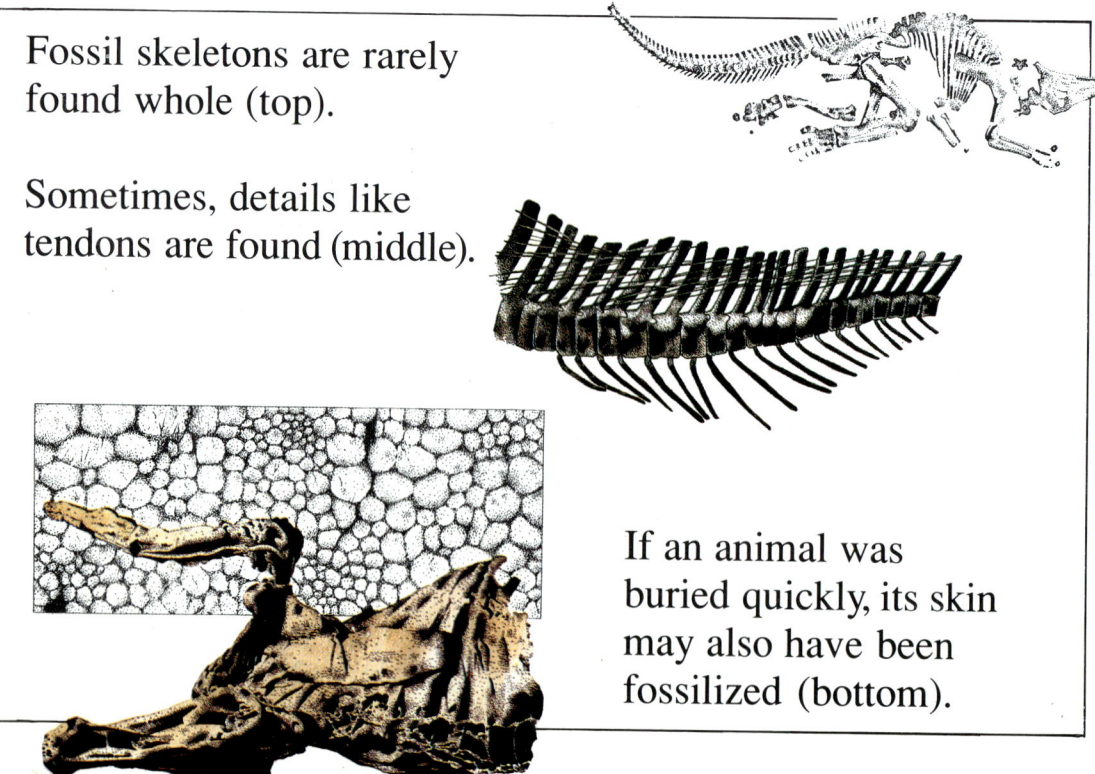

Fossil skeletons are rarely found whole (top).

Sometimes, details like tendons are found (middle).

If an animal was buried quickly, its skin may also have been fossilized (bottom).

Paleontologists piece bones together. These scientists look at related animals from the same time to see how they looked. Paleontologists also try to figure out how the muscles were attached to the bones. They then try to decide what the animal's skin was like and what color it was.

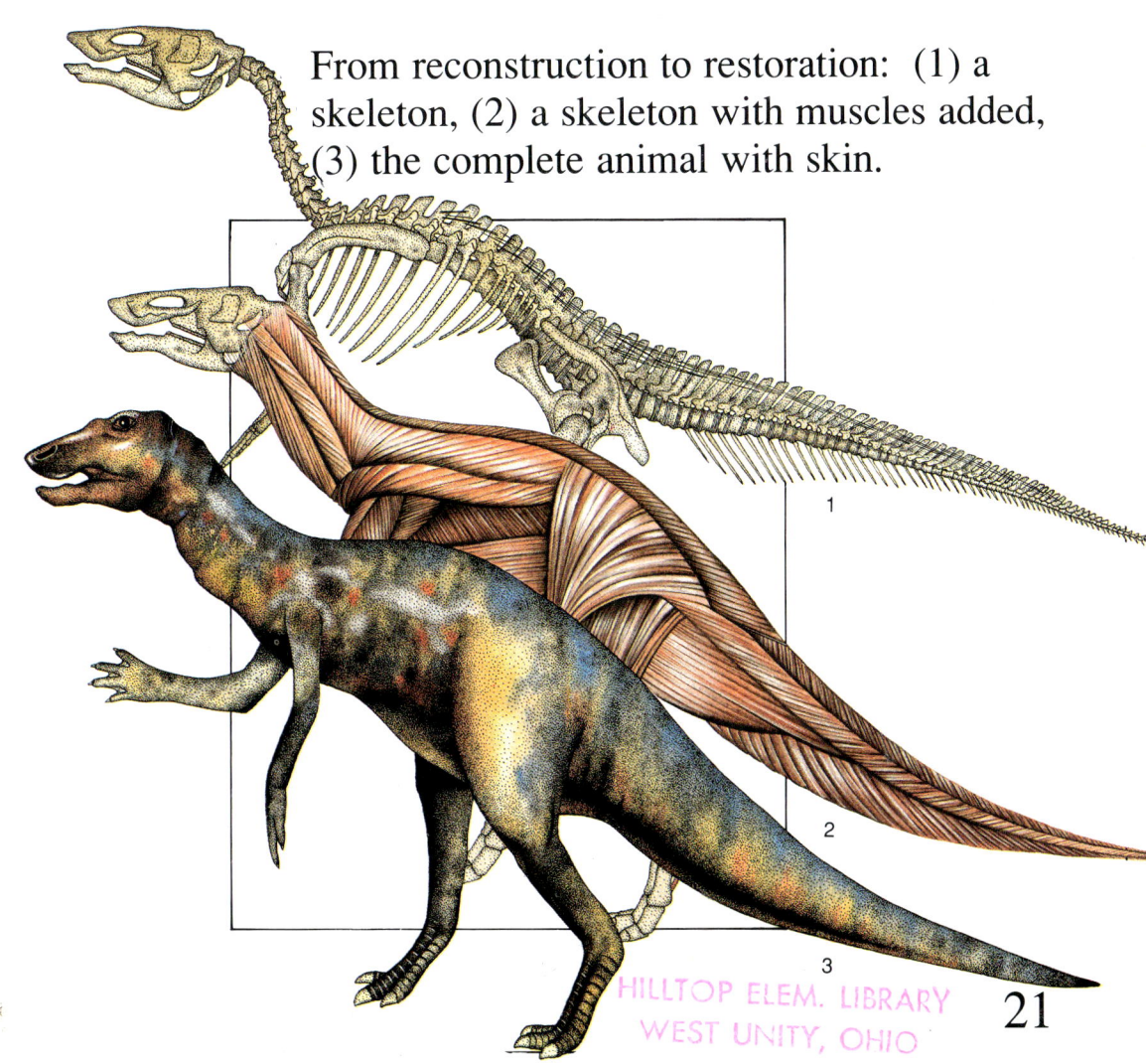

From reconstruction to restoration: (1) a skeleton, (2) a skeleton with muscles added, (3) the complete animal with skin.

A MUSEUM RESTORATION

1. A small model is made first.

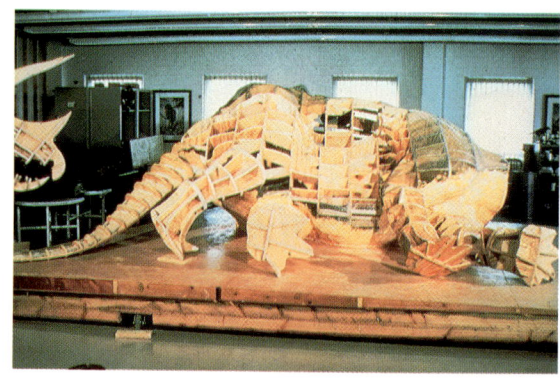

2. A large wood frame is built.

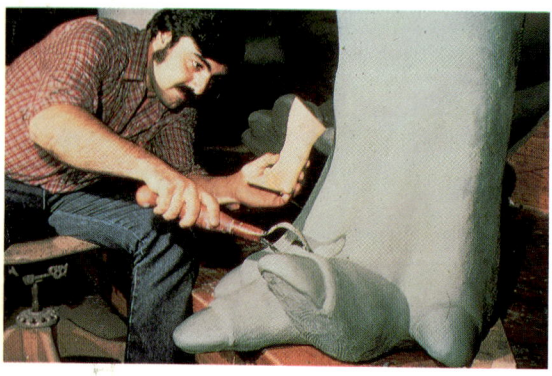

3. Clay is molded on the frame.

4. A mold is made from the clay, and then fiber glass is poured into the mold.

5. The final model is painted and placed with other animals.

6. The finished product: Tyrannosaurus eats Triceratops!

A PHOTOGRAPHIC RESTORATION

1

2

3

1. Jane Burton places a small model in front of a painted background.

2. She adjusts the background before taking the picture.

3. The finished photograph: a herd of Styracosaurus!

THE DISCOVERIES

By the mid-1800s, people had learned from fossils that enormous animals once roamed the Earth. British paleontologists named them Dinosauria, which means "terrible lizards."

In the United States, two scientists hunted for dinosaur bones. They were Othniel Charles Marsh and Edward Drinker Cope.

Othniel Charles Marsh (1831-1899) found many early dinosaur remains.

They hired teams to look for dinosaur bones. Marsh's team discovered 80 new species of dinosaurs. Cope's team found 56 new species.

Dinosaur remains have been found on every continent. They show us much about early animal and plant life. They also give us clues about how the continents may once have fit together.

Edward Drinker Cope (1840-1897) tried to find more fossils than Marsh.

Modern paleontologists have dug up many new types of fossilized reptiles. From these, we learn more and more about how dinosaurs lived. But one question is still unanswered: Why did the dinosaurs disappear?

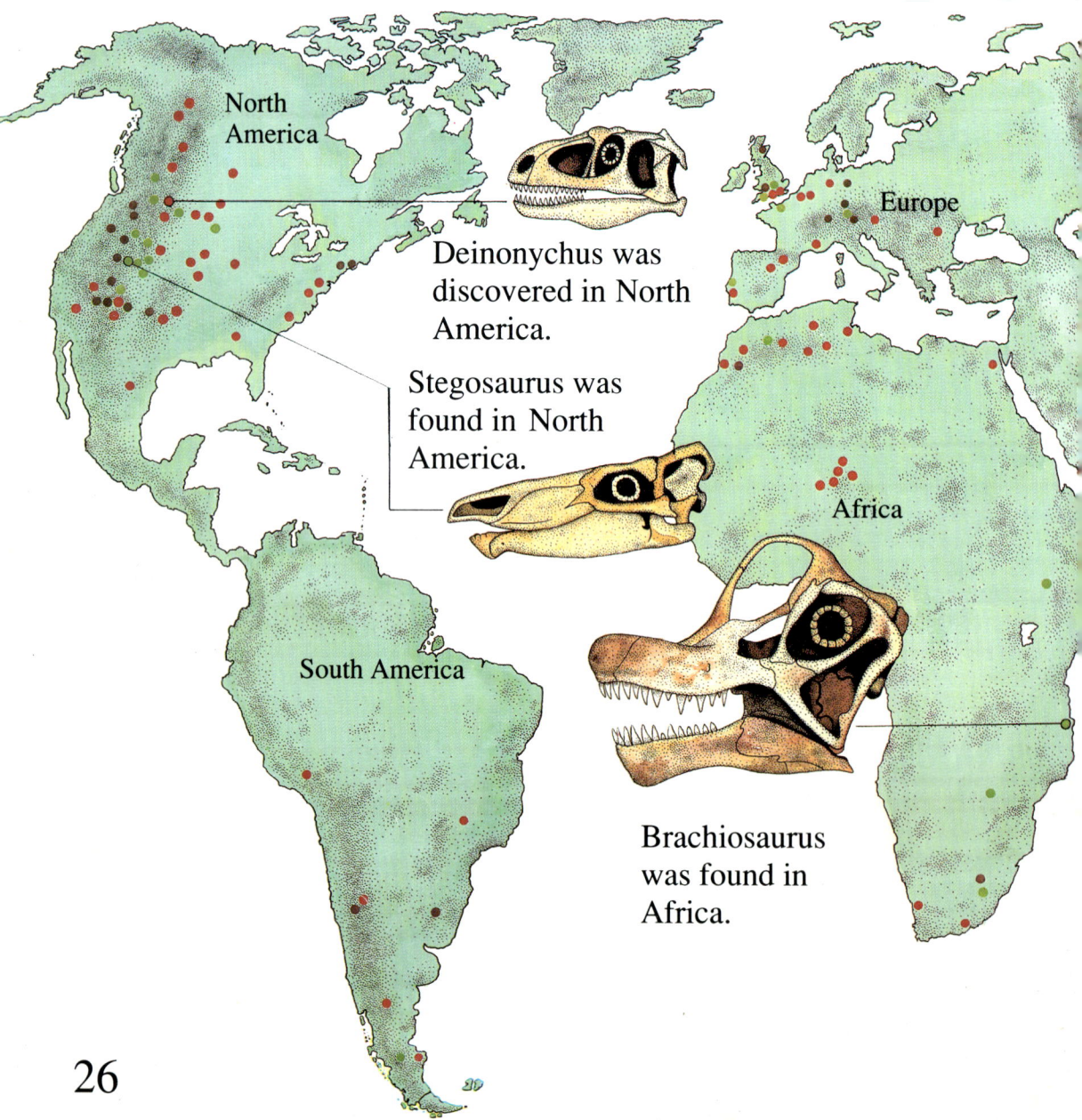

Deinonychus was discovered in North America.

Stegosaurus was found in North America.

Brachiosaurus was found in Africa.

Some scientists think a huge meteorite hit Earth. It would have stirred up dust that blocked the Sun for many years. Without light, many plants and animals would have died. But no one knows for sure what happened.

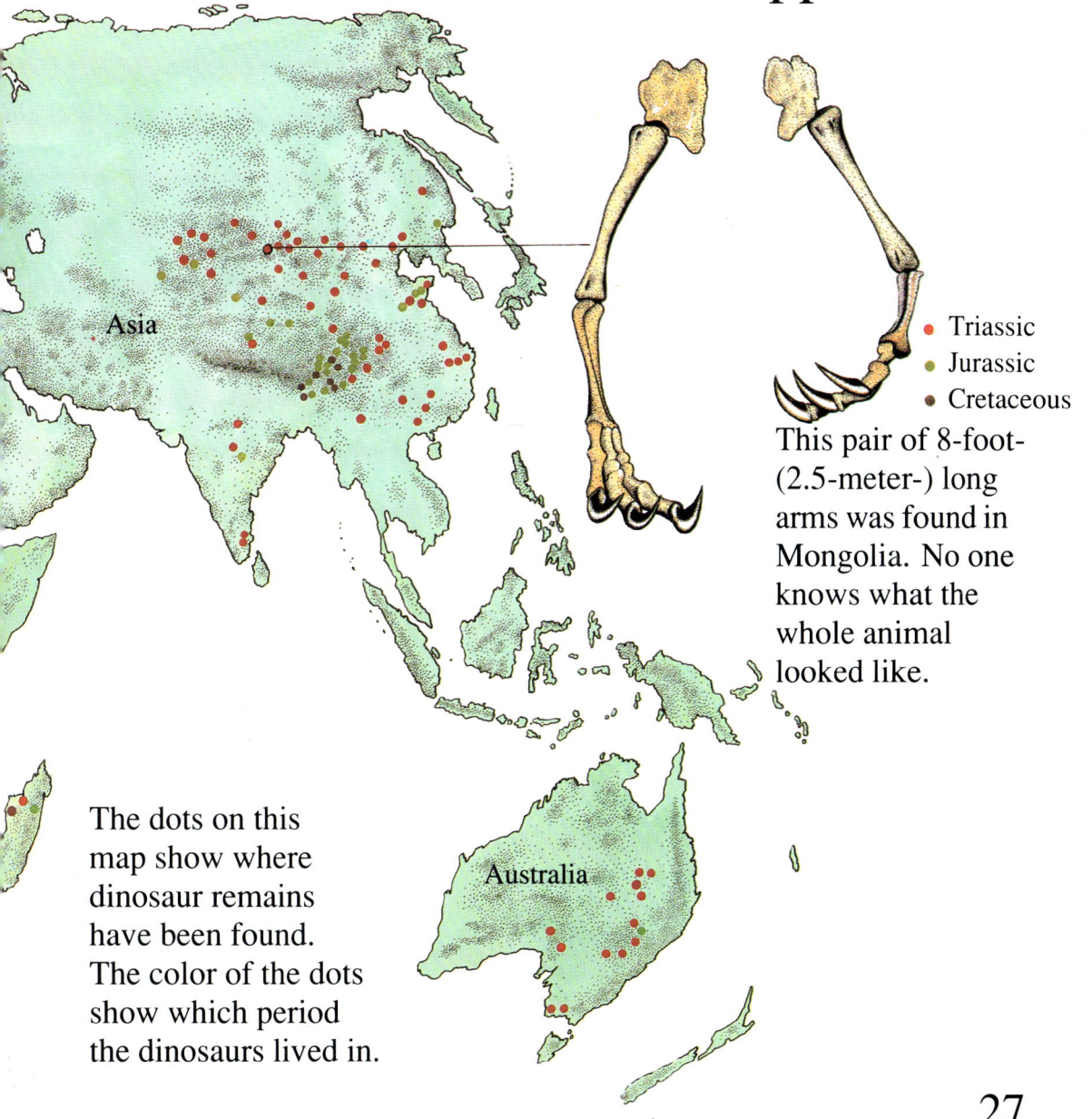

- Triassic
- Jurassic
- Cretaceous

This pair of 8-foot- (2.5-meter-) long arms was found in Mongolia. No one knows what the whole animal looked like.

The dots on this map show where dinosaur remains have been found. The color of the dots show which period the dinosaurs lived in.

27

Fun Facts about Dinosaur and Animal Life

1. Mary Anning discovered the first specimen of an ichthyosaur in 1811, when she was only 12 years old.

2. In 1878, 31 Iguanodon skeletons were discovered in a coal mine in Belgium. The whole herd had fallen into a ravine and become stuck in marshy ground.

3. The faster an animal runs, the farther apart its footprints become. From the size of a dinosaur's bones and the distance between its tracks, scientists can tell how fast it could run.

4. There are over 800 known types of dinosaurs. Scientists think there are even more to be discovered!

5. The least intelligent dinosaur was probably Diplodocus. It had the smallest brain compared to the size of its body.

6. Dinosaur eggs were probably no more than 12 inches (30.5 centimeters) long. Bigger eggs would need thicker shells or they would collapse. A larger dinosaur egg would have such a thick shell that the baby dinosaur would not be able to break out.

More Books about Dinosaurs

Here are more books about dinosaurs and other animals of their time.

Digging Up Dinosaurs.
   Aliki (Harper & Row)
Dinosaurs Are Different.
   Aliki (Harper & Row)

Where to See the Dinosaurs

Dinosaur State Park
Rocky Hill, Connecticut

Junior Museum
San Francisco,
   California

Museum of the Rockies
Bozeman, Montana

Zoological Gardens
Calgary, Alberta

Science Museum of
   Minnesota
St. Paul, Minnesota

Stovall Museum
Norman, Oklahoma

Dinosaur National Monument
Dinosaur, Colorado

Academy of Natural Sciences
Philadelphia, Pennsylvania

National Museum of Natural Sciences
Ottawa, Ontario

North Carolina Museum of Life and Science
Durham, North Carolina

New Words

adapt .... to change to fit different needs.

cold-blooded .... unable to control body temperature. The temperature of a cold-blooded animal changes with the temperature of its surroundings.

Cretaceous .... third and last period of the Age of Dinosaurs. It lasted from 135 million to 65 million years ago.

evolved .... changed its features over the centuries to suit its surroundings.

extinct .... died out, no longer existing.

fossils .... remains of animals or plants preserved in rock.

Jurassic .... second period of the Age of Dinosaurs. It lasted from 190 million to 135 million years ago.

mammal .... warm-blooded animal that bears live young.

paleontologist .... scientist who studies fossils.

reconstruction .... a skeleton of an animal that has been put together.

reptile .... cold-blooded animal that lays eggs on dry land.

restoration .... display showing what an entire animal looked like.

roam .... to wander.

streamlined .... built to make moving through air or water easier.

Triassic .... first period of the Age of Dinosaurs. It lasted from 225 million to 190 million years ago.

warm-blooded .... able to control body temperature.

Index and Pronunciation Guide

A
animals, early 10, 11

B
birds, early 15

D
Diplodocus
    (dip-LOD-uh-cus) 28

E
evolution 10, 11, 12

F
fish, early 10, 16
fossils 6, 8, 20, 24, 25,
    26, 27

H
humans 11

I
ichthyosaur
    (ICK-thee-oh-sawr) 28
Iguanodon
    (ih-GWAH-noh-don) 18,
    19, 28

M
mammals 11

P
paleontologists
    (pay-lee-on-TOL-oh-gists)
    6, 21, 24, 25, 26
plants, early 8, 9
Pterodactylus
    (TEHR-oh-DAC-teh-lus) 15

R
reconstruction 20, 21
reptiles 11, 12
restoration 20, 21, 22, 23

S
Stegosaurus
    (STEHG-oh-SAW-rus) 26
Styracosaurus
    (sty-RACK-oh-SAW-rus)
    23